NEPALI Alphabets

नेपाली अक्षरहरू

NEPALI Alphabets Picture Book with English Translations

This is a beautiful book for children of ages 4+ to learn NEPALI Alphabets both Vowels and Consonants

A NEPALI Alphabets Picture Book with English Translations.

The book details each alphabet, the English phonetics, the commonly used word in NEPALI, words English phonetics and its associated English word for easy understanding and reference with pictures.

- *Picture book details All 49 NEPALI ALPHABETS - 13 Nepali Vowels and 36 Nepali Consonants accompanied with a picture that describes the first words/sight words for respective alphabet*
- *A Perfect Bilingual Early Learning & Easy Teaching NEPALI Books for Kids*
- *The book features English phonetics, the commonly used word in NEPALI, words English phonetics and its associated English word*
- *Premium color cover design*
- *Printed on high quality perfectly sized pages at 8.5x11 inches COLOR pages*
- *Alphabets with commonly used word (NEPALI and English with phonetics) and pictures*

NEPALI VOWELS

Leave us your honest feedback and get your free download of NEPALI alphabet poster.

Email us at: Publishing@vaparisystems.com

avas in ask

अण्डा

Anda

Egg

aa, as in hat

आमा

Aama

Mother

i, as in ink

इन्द्रेणी

Indreni

Rainbow

ii,as in we

ईंटहरु

Iintaharu

Bricks

u, as in urge

Ullu

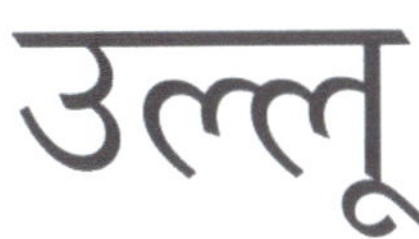

Owl

uu, as in noon

Uun

ऊन

Wool

ri, as in Rick

Ritu

Season

e, as in egg

एक

Ek

One

ai,as in mate

ऐना

Aina

Mirror

o, as in home

ओठ

Otha

Lips

au, as in house

औषधी

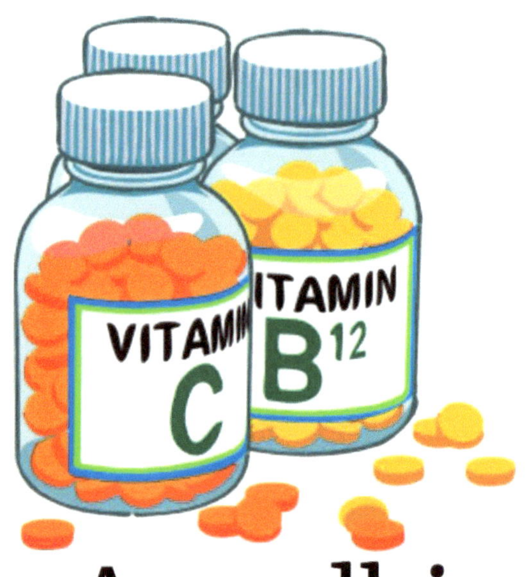

Auṣadhi

Medicine

am

अंगूर

Amgur

Grapes

अः

अः

ah

अः

अ अण्डा Egg	आ आमा Mother	इ इन्द्रेणी Rainbow	ई ईंटहरु Bricks
उ उल्लू Owl	ऊ ऊन Wool	ऋ ऋतु Season	ए एक One
ऐ ऐना Mirror	ओ ओठ Lips	औ औषधी Medicine	अं अंगूर Grapes
अः अः	NEPALI VOWELS नेपाली स्वर		

NEPALI CONSONANTS

Leave us your honest feedback and get your free download of NEPALI alphabet poster.

Email us at: Publishing@vaparisystems.com

[k]

Kamal

कमल

Lotus

[kha]

Kharayo

खरायो

Rabbit

[g]

गमला

gamala

Flowerpot

घ

[gha]

घर

Ghara

House

[nga]

नङ

Nanga

Nails

[ca]

चरा

Cara

Bird

[chha]

छाता

Chata

Umbrella

[ja]

जहाज

Jahaz

Ship

झ

[jha]

झण्डा

Jhaṇda

Flag

ञ

ञ

[nya]

ञ

ञ

[ta]

Tamatar

टमाटर

Tomato

[thh]

Ṭhannḍa

ठंण्डा

Cold

ड

[da]

डर

Ḍara

Fear

ढ

[dh]

ढोका

Ḍhōkā

Door

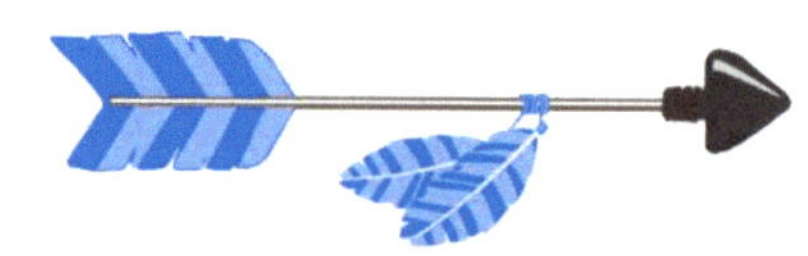

[n]

वाण

BaaN

Arrow

[t]

तरबूज

Tarabuja

WaterMelon

[tha]

थकान

Thakāna

Tiredness

[d]

दुइ

Dui

Two

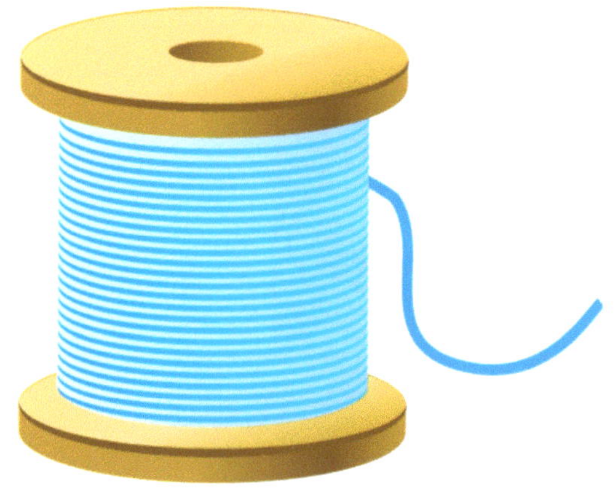

[dha]

धागो

Dhāgō

Thread

[na]

नल

Nal

Tap

[p]

पतंग

Pataṅga

Kite

[fa]

फल

Phala

Fruit

[b]

बज्यै

Bajyai

Grandma

[bha]

भकुन्डो

Bhakundo

Ball

[ma]

माछा

Māchа

Fish

[y]

योगी

Yogi

Yogi

[r]

रुपैया

Rupaiyā

Rupee

[la]

लसुन

Lasuna

Garlic

[v]

वन

Vana

Forest

[sha]

शब्दकोश

Shabdakosa

Dictionary

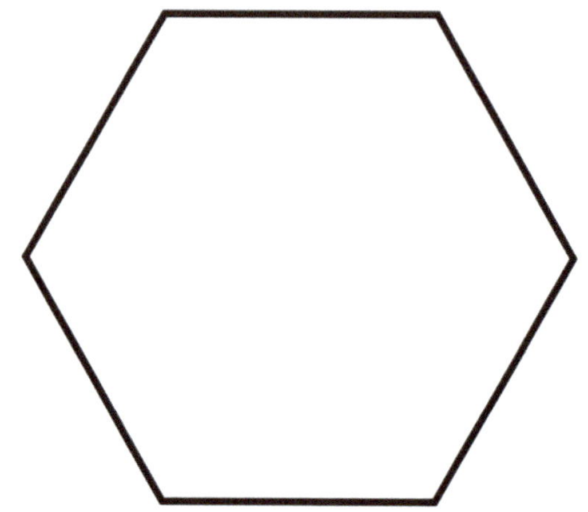

[shha]

षड्भुज

Hexagon

[sa]

स्याऊ

Syau

Apple

[ha]

हरिण

Harina

Deer

[kṣa]

क्षेत्री

Chhetri

Kshatriya

[tra]

त्रिशूल

Triśūla

Trishul

[jna]

ज्ञानी

Jñānī

Scholar

www.ingramcontent.com/pod-product-compliance
Ingram Content Group UK Ltd.
Pitfield, Milton Keynes, MK11 3LW, UK
UKHW060107300726
14090UKWH00003B/399

* 9 7 9 8 4 2 3 2 5 5 1 2 1 *